Pebble® Plus

**Physical Science**

# Sound

by Abbie Dunne

CAPSTONE PRESS
a capstone imprint

**Pebble Plus is published by Capstone Press,**
1710 Roe Crest Drive, North Mankato, Minnesota 56003
www.mycapstone.com

**Library of Congress Cataloging-in-Publication Data**
Names: Dunne, Abbie, author.
Title: Sound / by Abbie Dunne.
Description: North Mankato, Minnesota : Capstone Press, [2017] | Series:
    Pebble plus. Physical science | Audience: Ages 4-8. | Audience: K to
    grade 3. | Includes bibliographical references and index.
Identifiers: LCCN 2016005332| ISBN 9781515709404 (library binding) | ISBN
    9781515709725 (pbk.) | ISBN 9781515711070 (ebook (pdf))
Subjects: LCSH: Sound--Juvenile literature. | Hearing—Juvenile literature.
Classification: LCC QC225.5 .D86 2017 | DDC 534—dc23
LC record available at http://lccn.loc.gov/2016005332

**Editorial Credits**
Linda Staniford, editor; Veronica Scott, designer; Eric Gohl, media researcher;
Katy LaVigne, production specialist

**Photo Credits**
Getty Images: KidStock/Blend Images, 15; Shutterstock: anekoho, 13, Asier Romero, 9, Luis Molinero, 11, Mark Herreid, 19, MNI, 7, Ollyy, cover, snapgalleria, 17, Tommaso Lizzul, 5, Winston Link, 21

Design Elements: Shutterstock

**Note to Parents and Teachers**
The Physical Science set supports national curriculum standards for science. This book introduces the concept of sound. The images support early readers in understanding the text. The repetition of words and phrases helps early readers in understanding the text. This book also introduces early readers to subject-specific vocabulary words, which are defined in the Glossary section. Early readers may need assistance to read some words and to use the Table of Contents, Glossary, Read More, Internet Sites, Critical Thinking Using the Common Core, and Index sections of the book.

Printed and bound in China.
007701

# Table of Contents

## What is Sound?

Sound is made up of waves.
Sound waves are made
when something vibrates.
The vibrating object sends
waves into the air.

The vibrations move through air
like ripples on a pond.
This is how sound waves spread.
We can't see sound waves,
but we can hear them.

## How do Sound Waves Travel?

Sound waves spread out in all directions. They bounce back if they hit something solid, such as a wall. The waves stop if they hit something that absorbs them.

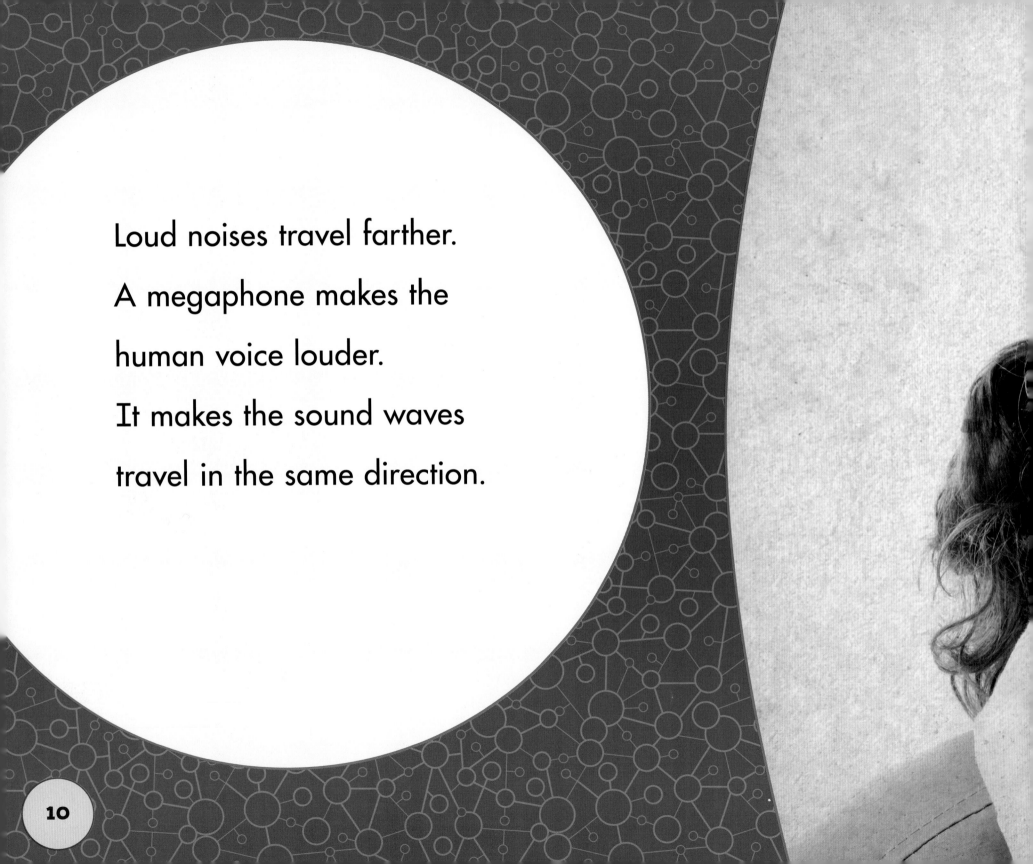

Loud noises travel farther.
A megaphone makes the
human voice louder.
It makes the sound waves
travel in the same direction.

## Making Sounds

There are many ways
to make sounds. You can
tap, rub, or scrape one object
against another. Machines make
noises as their parts move.

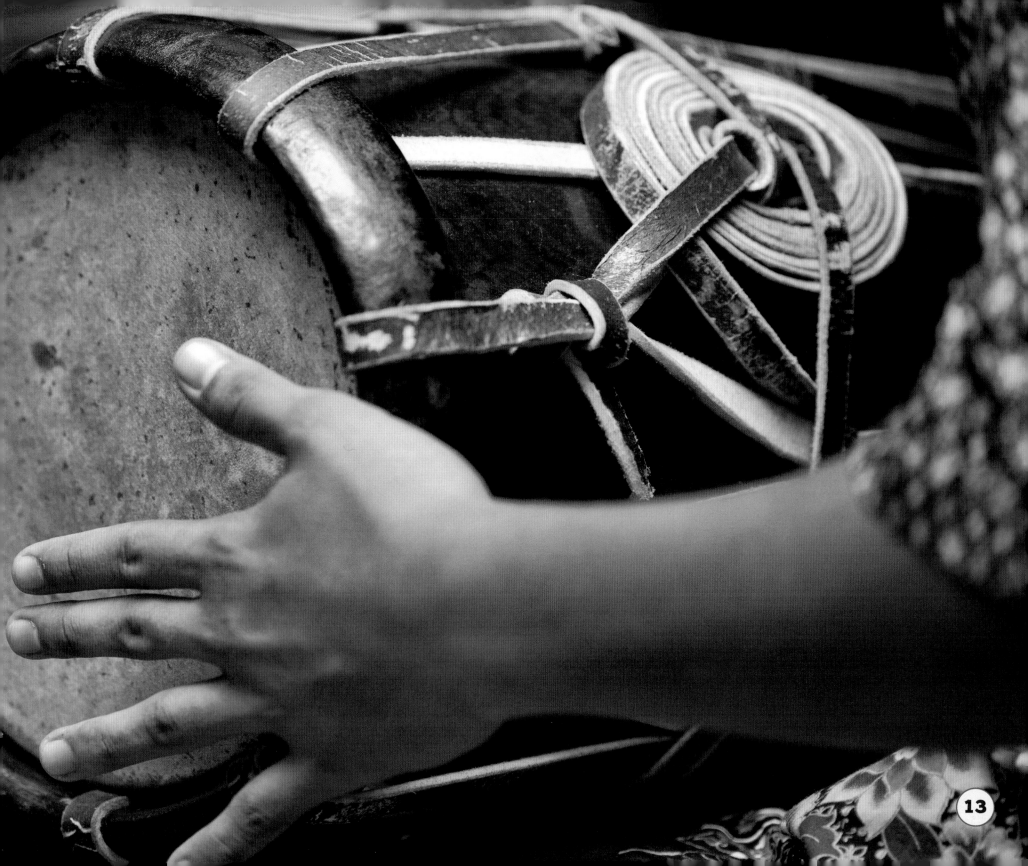

Different musical instruments make different sounds. Some are blown. Others are struck. Some have strings that are plucked or scraped.

## How We Hear Sound

Your ear catches sound waves.
The waves move inside
your ear. The sound waves
make your eardrum vibrate.
A nerve sends sound to the brain.

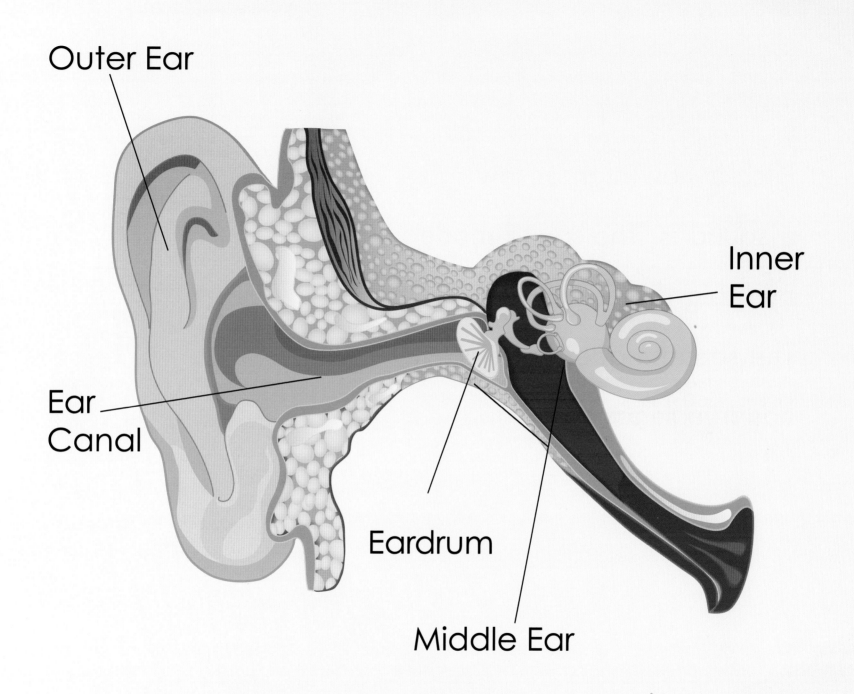

Outer Ear

Inner
Ear

Ear
Canal

Eardrum

Middle Ear

17

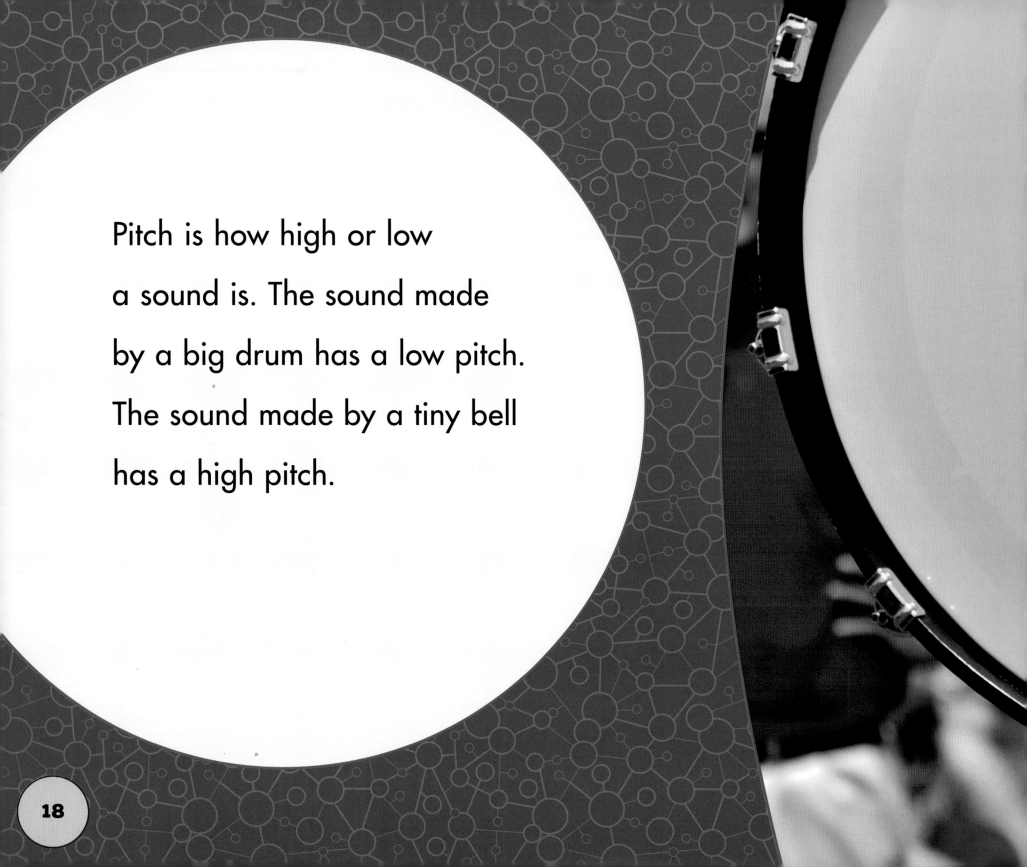

Pitch is how high or low a sound is. The sound made by a big drum has a low pitch. The sound made by a tiny bell has a high pitch.

# Activity

## Investigating Vibrations and Sound

How can you show that vibrations make sound and that sound makes things vibrate? Follow the steps below to find out.

## What You Need

- drum, or a drum made by stretching a balloon across the top of a lidless can
- 2 pencils or drumsticks
- paper
- grains of rice

## What You Do

1. Beat the drum with the pencils or drumsticks.

2. Make notes about what you hear and see.

3. Now place the grains of rice on the drum. Beat the drum with the pencils again.

4. Make notes about what you hear and see.

## What Do You Think?

Make claims.

Claims are things you believe to be true. How did you show that vibrations make sound and that sound makes things vibrate?

Use what you saw while beating the drum with and without the rice to support your claims.

# Glossary

**eardrum**—a thin piece of skin stretched tight like a drum inside the ear; the eardrum vibrates when sound waves strike it

**megaphone**—an instrument used to make the voice sound louder

**nerve**—a thin fibre that carries messages between the brain and other parts of the body

**pitch**—how high or low a sound is

**sound wave**—a wave or vibration that can be heard

**vibrate**—to move back and forth quickly

# Read More

**Boothroyd, Jennifer.** *Vibrations Make Sound.* First Step Nonfiction: Light and Sound. Minneapolis: Lerner Publications Company, 2015.

**Navarro, Paula.** *Surprising Experiments with Sound.* Magic Science. New York: Barron's Educational Series, 2014.

**Royston, Angela.** *All About Sound.* All About Science. Chicago: Heinemann Raintree, 2016.

# Internet Sites

FactHound offers a safe, fun way to find Internet sites related to this book. All of the sites on FactHound have been researched by our staff.

Here's all you do:

Visit *www.facthound.com*

Type in this code: 9781515709404

Check out projects, games and lots more at
**www.capstonekids.com**

# Critical Thinking Using the Common Core

1. What happens to a sound wave when it hits a wall?
   (Key Ideas and Details)

2. Explain what vibrations are.
   (Key Ideas and Details)

3. If you blow strongly into a recorder, and then blow gently, do you think the sounds you make will be different?
   (Integration of Knowledge and Ideas)

# Index